Answers

W0013467
9781382054003

Explanations in the main text of the book are referred to by their page.

Learning Paper: Synonyms

1 **remedy, cure** Both words mean a solution to a medical problem or illness.
2 **disturb, upset** Both words mean to disrupt.
3 **demand, insist** Both words mean to ask for something strongly.
4 **area, region** Both words mean a particular district.
5 **begin** Both 'start' and 'begin' mean to commence something.
6 **fright** Both 'fear' and 'fright' mean an anxiety or horror about something.
7 **alter, change** Both mean to make something different.
8 **fidget, wriggle** Both mean to move restlessly.
9 **hard, difficult** Both mean challenging.
10 **band**
11 **rough**
12 **sweet**
13 **flat** 'Flat' means level and even; it also refers to somewhere you can live like an apartment or rooms.
14 **key** A 'key' to a puzzle means the same as a clue or a lead; 'key' is also an adjective meaning central or important.
15 **orange** 'Orange' is a colour (like red and yellow) and also a fruit (like apple and grape).
16 **bill** If you are paying a 'bill', you are paying a price for something that has been supplied; a 'bill' on a bird is a beak or snout.
17 **rock** A 'rock' is a stone or boulder; 'rock' is also a verb meaning to sway or move.
18 **hail** All the words are types of rain, frozen or otherwise.
19 **stable** All the words denote homes or shelters for animals.
20 **carrots** All the words are vegetables.
21 **speak** All the words are verbs related to speech.
22 **toddlers** All the words are nouns for children or young people.
23 di<u>ffi</u>cult
24 co<u>ar</u>se
25 rel<u>ax</u>ed

Learning Paper: Antonyms

1 **sell, purchase** 'Purchase' means to buy which is the opposite of 'sell'.
2 **dim, bright** If a light is 'dim' it is difficult to see. A 'bright' light is very clear.
3 **question, answer** A 'question' is when something is asked. An 'answer' is the explanation.
4 **accept, refuse** To 'accept' is to say yes to something. To 'refuse' is to say no.
5 **start** To 'quit' is to leave or stop whereas 'start' is to begin.
6 **calm** 'Panic' is anxiety or lack of control whereas 'calm' is 'peace'.
7 **help** To 'hinder' is to prevent' whereas to 'help' means to assist.
8 **first** 'Last' means final whereas 'first' means initial.
9 **cheap** 'Cheap' means not costing a lot whereas 'expensive' means the opposite.
10 **part** 'Whole' is complete whereas a 'part' is a section of something.

11 **fail** To succeed is to attain a goal. To 'fail' is to fall short.
12 **west** 'East' and 'west' are opposite sides of a compass or weathervane.
13 **shiny, dull** 'Shiny' is the most opposite to 'dull' because 'shiny' means bright whereas 'dull' means without shine.
14 **generous, mean** If one is 'generous' one is open-handed. 'Mean' means miserly, penny-pinching and ungenerous.
15 **home, away** If you play a match at 'home' you play it on your home ground. If you play 'away', the match takes place at your opponents' ground.
16 **often, seldom** 'Often' means frequently whereas 'seldom' means rarely.
17 **raise, lower** 'Raise' means to lift up and 'lower' means to take down.
18–20 **hammer C, fork G, spade G, dollar M, trowel G, cent M**
21 **road, path** The other words are types of dwellings.
22 **swim, dive** The other words are items of clothing.
23 **kneel, sit** The other words involve moving from one place to another.
24 **butter, flour** The other words are things that can be baked.
25 **apple, plum** The other words are vegetables.

Learning Paper: Finding Words and Letters

1 **ever** This book can b<u>e ver</u>y useful.
2 **rear** The<u>re ar</u>e fairies at the bottom of the garden.
3 **soft** This house i<u>s oft</u>en cold.
4 **ends** Will the journey <u>end s</u>oon?
5 **e** made, error   6 **k** risk, king
7 **t** list, then   8 **t** foot, trade
9 **f** cuff, fringe; myself, fruit
10 **w** willow, wand; snow, west
11 **b** brow, black, beast, brake, bat
12 **f** flush, feast, fear, flung, fearful
13 **after** afternoon, aftercare, aftertaste, afterthought
14 **motor** motorbike, motorcar, motorway, motorboat
15 **grass**   16 **knife**
17 **AIR** chairs   19 **FRIGHT**
18 **CAT** caterpillar 20 **CREAM**
21 **SIRE**   22 **TALE**
23 **cloudy** The colourful kite fluttered in the breeze.
24 **has** Please may I have a red balloon? Or May I have a red balloon, please?
25 **letter** The postman always slams our gate shut.

Learning Paper: Sorting Words and Letters

1 **beak** Each word can be applied to some birds, but all birds have beaks.
2 **trees** A forest, by definition, always has trees.
3 <u>**closed**</u>, **opened** As it was hot and stuffy, I opened my bedroom window.
4 <u>**raincoat**</u>, **towel** After swimming, I dried myself on my towel.
5 **PLATE, PETAL**
6 **SHORE, HORSE**
7 **BEGIN**   8 **BELOW**   9 **CHEAP**
10 **nameless**   11 **behead**   12 **textbook**

13 **farmer, shed, milk the cows**
14 **spade, beach, castle**
15 **forget, post, letter**
16 **lantern, face, buried**
17 As **it** is cold I am wearing **tights**.
18 I'm sorry **I've** broken the **glass**.
19 I'll **have** to get him **home**.
20 **erase** There is no 's' in 'terrace'.
21 **stead** There is no 'e' in 'distant'.
22 **tramp** There is no 'm' in 'painter'.
23 **large**   24 **staid**   25 **rinse**

Learning Paper: Substitution, Number and Logic

1 **E** $8 - 3 = 5; 5 = E$
2 **B** $6 \div 2 = 3; 3 = B$
3 **B** $(5 + 4) - 6 = 9 - 6 = 3; 3 = B$
4 **D** $2 \times 2 = 4; 4 = D$
5 **E** $2 + 3 = 5; 5 = E$
6 **2** $18 \div 6 = 3$ and $20 \div 4 = 5$, so $16 \div 8 = 2$
7 **24** $2 \times 9 = 18$ and $3 \times 4 = 12$, so $6 \times 4 = 24$
8 **15** $11 + 3 = 14$ and $5 + 0 = 5$, so $8 + 7 = 15$
9 **64** $10 \times 10 = 100$ and $4 \times 4 = 16$, so $8 \times 8 = 64$
10 **1** $13 - 11 = 2$ and $10 - 4 = 6$, so $9 - 8 = 1$
11–12 In order of working:
$R = 96$
$G = 100 - 5 = 95$
$D = 95 - 7 = 88$
$S = 96 - 12 = 84$
$M = 96 - (96 \div 2) = 48$
M = 48, G = 95, D = 88, S = 84
13 **Guitars are stringed instruments.** This is supported by the statement, 'Guitars are musical instruments. Guitars have strings.'
14 **Houses are popular.** This is supported by the statement, 'People like living in houses.' The other sentences may be true but are not supported by the information given.
15–19 Refer to pages 25–30 on Substitution, Number and Logic and pages 43–45 on Alphabetical Order (Curveball Question 1). Arrange the words in a grid to make it easier to put them in alphabetical order.

15 **baby**

b	a	b	y						
g	r	o	w	n	u	p			
p	e	n	s	i	o	n	e	r	
s	c	h	o	o	l	g	i	r	l
s	t	u	d	e	n	t			

16 **seedling**

b	u	d					
f	l	o	w	e	r		
l	e	a	f				
s	e	e	d				
s	e	e	d	l	i	n	g

17 **pushchair**

b	i	c	y	c	l	e		
c	a	r						
p	r	a	m					
p	u	s	h	c	h	a	i	r
t	r	i	c	y	c	l	e	

18 **letter**

b	o	o	k					
l	e	t	t	e	r			
p	a	r	a	g	r	a	p	h
s	e	n	t	e	n	c	e	
w	o	r	d					

19 **quadruple**

d	o	u	b	l	e			
n	o	n	e					
q	u	a	d	r	u	p	l	e
s	i	n	g	l	e			
t	r	i	p	l	e			

20 **B** BANANA = AAA**B**NN, so the fourth is B.

21

C	O	U	R	T
O	■	S	■	I
M	■	H	■	M
I	■	E	■	I
C	A	R	E	D

22

E	A	R	L	Y
V	■	E	■	A
A	■	A	■	C
D	■	D	■	H
E	G	Y	P	T

23

M	A	D	A	M
U	■	E	■	A
S	■	L	■	J
I	■	V	■	O
C	L	E	A	R

24

P	U	S	H	Y
I	■	T	■	■
P	R	O	V	E
I	■	R	■	■
T	R	E	A	T

25

R	I	P	E	R
■	■	L	■	I
M	E	A	L	S
■	■	N	■	E
M	O	T	O	R

Learning Papers

Learning Paper: Word Progressions

1 **b** ear, blink
2 **e** clan, breathe
3 **l** and, flake
4 **d** one, dwell
5 **l** spice, slides
6 **bend** The pattern here is to replace 'a' with 'e' in the second word.
7 **wail** The pattern here is to replace 's' with 'w' in the second word.
8 **vole** The pattern here is to swap the first and third letters.
9 **dale** The pattern here is to move the second letter to the end of the word.
10 **heir** The pattern here is to move the fourth letter to become the second letter.
11 **tree**
12 **lean**
13 **sand**
14 **fame**
15 **spin**
16 **REAL**

	3	1		2		4		3	1			2		4	
H	E	R	B	A	S	K	S	A	J	A	R	E	E	L	S

17 **NEST**

	1	2		3	4				1	2		3	4		
C	I	T	Y	P	E	A	S	B	O	N	E	S	T	I	R

18 **FOUL**

	2	3		4		2?	1		2?	3		4		2?	1
M	A	I	L	T	H	A	W	S	O	U	R	L	E	A	F

19 **BEDS**

4	1				2	3		4	1				2	3	
E	N	D	S	I	C	O	N	S	O	B	S	E	D	G	E

20 **TOOK**

	2	3		4			1		2	3		4			I
T	I	N	S	D	R	A	B	W	O	O	D	K	I	L	T

21 **SAND**
22 **MAKE**
23 **DEAL**
24 **BALL**
25 **COME**

Learning Paper: Codes

1 **e d a b** M = e, A = d, S = a and T = b
2 **b d e c** T = b, A = d, M = e and E = c
3 **MESS** e = M, c = E and a = S
4 **MATE** e = M, d = A, b = T and c = E
5 **647352** A = 6, N = 4, T = 7, L = 3, E = 5, R = 2
6 **PLANE** 8 = P, 3 = L, 6 = A, 4 = N, 5 = E
7 **PLEAT** 8 = P, 3 = L, 5 = E, 6 = A, 7 = T
8 **£ : ! *** P = £, O = :, R = !, T = *
9 **/ ! : £** C = /, R = !, O = :, P = £
10 **ERECT** ? = E, ! = R, ? = E, / = C, * = T
11 **CHEAT** * = C, z = H, 7 = E, y = A, % = T
12 **TRACE** % = T, B = R, y = A, * = C, 7 = E
13–17 Start with the letter R. Two of the words begin with R, thus R = 7. Three of the words end with K, thus K = 9. All the words can now be matched with their correct codes.
13 **7359** R = 7, I = 3, N = 5, K = 9
14 **7159** R = 7, A = 1, N = 5, K = 9
15 **359** I = 3, N = 5, K = 9
16 **935** K = 9, I = 3, N = 5
17 **5617** N = 5, E = 6, A = 1, R = 7
18–22 One of the words has only three letters so you can immediately match TEA to 4 3 2. Now you know these letters, you can identify all the codes including the missing one.
18 **7 2 1 4** M = 7, A = 2, S = 1, T = 4
19 **1 4 2 5** S = 1, T = 4, A = 2, R = 5
20 **5 3 1 4** R = 5, E = 3, S = 1, T = 4
21 **4 3 2** T = 4, E = 3, 2 = A
22 **5 3 2 7** R = 5, E = 3, A = 2, M = 7
23–25 Two of the words begin 'PL' so one of those word's codes is missing. 'LEAP' ends in a 'P' so looking at the codes 'P' must = q. Therefore, m * 4 q = LEAP. PLEA uses exactly the same letters as LEAP in a different order so you can see that PLAN must be q m 4 k and you can work out PLEA.
23 **qm*4** P = q, L = m, E = *, A = 4
24 **qm4k** P = q, L = m, A = 4, N = k
25 **m*4q** L = m, E = *, A = 4, P = q

Learning Paper: Sequences

1 **April, May** 'April' is the month before 'May' in the same way as 'Tuesday' is the day before 'Wednesday'.
2 **lamb, sheep** A 'lamb' is a young 'sheep' in the same way as a 'puppy' is a young 'dog'.
3 **artist, picture** An 'artist' creates a 'picture' in the same way as an author writes a 'book'.
4 **cup, drink** One 'drinks' out of a 'cup' as one 'eats' off a 'plate'.
5 **uncle, nephew** 'Uncle' is the same relation to a 'nephew' as 'aunt' is to a 'niece'.
6 **GH** The second pair is the next two letters in the alphabet after the first pair.
7 **JL** Each letter in the first pair moves forwards three places in the second pair.
8 **P8** The letter in the first pair moves forwards one place in the second pair. The number in the first pair increases by 2 in the second pair.
9 **18BC** The number in the first pair increases by 3 in the second pair. The letters remain the same.
10 **2DE** The number in the first pair decreases by 2 in the second pair. The letters in the first pair move forwards one place in the second pair.
11 **AL, BM** The first letter in each pairing is a repeated pattern: ABABAB. The second letter moves forwards one place.
12 **BA, DC** Each letter in a pair moves forwards two places.
13 **NC, LX** The first letter moves backwards two places. The second letter is a repeating pattern: CXCXCX.
14 **GiH, KmN** The first capital letter moves forwards two places each time. The lower case letter moves forwards two places each time. The third letter (capital) moves forwards three places each time.
15 **NM, OL** The first letter in each pair moves forwards one place each time. The second letter moves back one place each time.
16 **82, 55** Each number in the sequence decreases by 9.
17 **½, 1** Each number in the sequence increases by

one quarter.

18 **63, 56** Each number in the sequence decreases by 7.
19 **99, 110** Each number in the sequence increases by 11.
20 **11, 16** The number added increases each time: +1, +2, +3, +4, +5.
21 **CN35, DO25** The first letter in each pair is in a sequence of two: BB, CC, DD. The second letter moves forward one place each time. The numbers decrease by 10 each time.
22 **5R, 17Z** The number in each group increases by 3 each time. The letter in each group moves forward by two letters each time.
23 **Z9A, W6D** The first letter in each group moves back by one letter each time. The second letter in each group moves forward by one letter each time. The number in the middle of each group decreases by 1 each time.
24 **VR9, XN9** The first letter in each group moves forward by one letter each time. The second letter in each group moves back by two letters each time. The number is a repeating pattern: 9, 6, 9, 6, 9, 6 so the missing numbers are both 9s.
25 **GfH, HgJ** The first letter in each trio moves forward by one letter each time. The second letter, which is lower case, also moves forward by one letter at a time. The third letter in each trio, moves forward by two letters.

Curveball Questions 1: Alphabetical Order

1 **S** AEH**S**TUX
2 **house**

H	O	N	E	Y
H	O	U	N	D
H	O	U	R	S
H	O	U	S	E
H	U	M	A	N

3 **SUSPECT** 'S' is the nineteenth letter; 'T' is the twentieth letter.
4 **ZEBRA** Z = twenty-sixth, E = fifth, B = second, R = eighteenth and A = first letter.
5 **R** HHM**R**TY
6 **previous**

P	R	E	V	I	O	U	S	
P	R	E	T	T	Y			
P	R	E	E	N				
P	R	E	C	I	S	E		
P	R	E	C	I	P	I	C	E
P	R	E	C	I	O	U	S	

7 **SPOON** S = nineteenth, P = sixteenth, O = fifteenth, O = fifteenth and N = fourteenth letter.
8 **reason**

P	A	R	A	D	E
P	A	T	R	O	L
R	E	A	D	E	R
R	E	A	S	O	N
R	E	G	I	O	N

9 **N** EI**N**OQSTU
10 **H** ABEG**H**MRRU
11 **HIPPO** 'H' is the eighth letter; 'O' is the fifteenth letter.
12 **beach**
13 **chivalry**

C	H	O	R	U	S		
C	H	I	V	A	L	R	Y
C	H	E	M	I	S	T	
C	H	A	R	A	D	E	
C	H	A	M	B	E	R	

14 **frostbite**

F	R	O	W	N				
F	R	O	S	T	B	I	T	E
F	R	I	E	N	D			
F	R	I	C	T	I	O	N	
F	R	A	C	T	I	O	N	

15 **trellis**

T	R	O	P	H	Y			
T	R	E	L	L	I	S		
T	R	E	A	S	U	R	E	
T	R	A	M	P	O	L	I	N	E
T	R	A	I	N				

16 **hedge**
17 **DANCE** D = fourth, A = first, N = fourteenth, C = third and E = fifth letter.
18 **customary, cushion, curable, cupboard, culture, culinary**

C	U	S	T	O	M	A	R	Y
C	U	S	H	I	O	N		
C	U	R	A	B	L	E		
C	U	P	B	O	A	R	D	
C	U	L	T	U	R	E		
C	U	L	I	N	A	R	Y	

19 **JUNIOR** 'J' is the tenth letter; 'R' is the eighteenth.
20 **S** AEEMNS**S**SST
21 **slowly**

Y	L	D	N	E	I	R	F
Y	L	I	P	P	A	H	
Y	L	L	A	M	R	O	N
Y	L	T	F	O	S		
Y	L	W	O	L	S		

22 **showed**

D	E	C	A	L	P	S	I	M
D	E	C	N	A	L	G		
D	E	G	R	A	H	C		
D	E	H	S	I	L	O	P	

D	E	W	O	H	S			

23 truth

H	T	F	I	F					
H	T	I	M	S	K	C	A	L	B
H	T	L	A	E	H				
H	T	M	R	A	W				
H	T	U	R	T					

24 satin

N	I	A	T	P	A	C		
N	I	A	T	R	E	T	N	E
N	I	L	E	V	A	J		
N	I	M	A	T	I	V		
N	I	T	A	S				

25 confront

T	N	A	C	A	V		
T	N	E	D	I	C	C	A
T	N	E	R	A	P		
T	N	E	S	B	A		
T	N	O	R	F	N	O	C

Mixed Paper 1

1–5 Refer to pages 8–11 on Synonyms.
1 **power**
2 **coast**
3 **herd**
4 **collar**
5 **clock**

6–25 Refer to pages 15–19 on Finding Words and Letters.
6 **BUTTER**
7 **GRUBBY**
8 **ELEPHANT**
9 **LITTER**
10 **ENVELOPES**
11 **AND** hands
12 **RIP** dripping
13 **FUN** funny
14 **ARK** darker
15 **EAR** hearing
16 **BAT**
17 **COST**
18 **EVER**
19 **PANE**
20 **SING**
21 **oval** Not only is the stamp attractive but it is als<u>o val</u>uable.
22 **were** It was the tallest to<u>wer e</u>ver seen.
23 **rope** My poor mother had fou<u>r ope</u>rations.
24 **itch** Izzy's rabb<u>it ch</u>ewed a hole in her hutch.
25 **tone** Well done, you're the las<u>t one</u> out.

26–30 Refer to pages 31–34 on Word Progressions.
26 **b** ear, blink
27 **l** pan, flit
28 **l** and, flake
29 **d** one, dwell
30 **t** sun, petal

31–35 Refer to pages 20–24 on Sorting Words and Letters. Try each of the words in the first set of brackets. Do they make sense with any words in the second and third set of brackets? Only one combination of three words makes sense.
31 **shirt, football, team**
32 **sharpener, bag, chair**
33 **ship, harbour, slowly**
34 **listened, hear, coming**
35 **Antarctic, huge, houses**

36–35 Refer to pages 25–30 on Substitution, Number and Logic.
36–40 Solve these questions by looking at the first set of three and working out how the first and last numbers have been used to arrive at the middle number. Apply this to the second set of three and see if it works. If it does, apply it to the last set.
36 **29** $11 + 12 = 23$ and $6 + 9 = 15$, so $18 + 11 = 29$
37 **14** $25 - 6 = 19$ and $17 - 7 = 10$, so $23 - 9 = 14$
38 **1** $14 \div 7 = 2$ and $33 \div 11 = 3$, so $6 \div 6 = 1$
39 **24** $(3 \times 5) \times 2 = 30$ and $(7 \times 3) \times 2 = 42$, so $(6 \times 2) \times 2 = 12 \times 2 = 24$
40 **72** $8 \times 3 = 24$ and $6 \times 5 = 30$, so $9 \times 8 = 72$

41

S	■	■	■	M
T	E	N	S	E
I	■	O	■	T
F	E	N	C	E
F	■	E	■	R

42

T	I	M	E	R
R	■	O	■	E
E	■	T	■	A
A	■	O	■	C
T	O	R	C	H

43

H	O	R	S	E
E	■	■	■	R
A	M	B	L	E
P	■	■	■	C
S	P	O	R	T

44

T	■	F	■	L
O	■	U	■	A
W	A	N	D	S
E	■	N	■	E
L	A	Y	E	R

45–49 Refer to pages 20–24 on Sorting Words and Letters.
45 **STONE**
46 **DARE**
47 **SHRUB**
48 **CRATE**
49 **REAR**

50–54 Refer to pages 35–38 on Codes.
50 **PIE** $2 = P$, $1 = I$ and $4 = E$

51 **KIN** 7 = K, 8 = I and 6 = N
52 **ARE** 3 = A, 4 = R and 2 = E
53 **PAW** 6 = P, 1 = A and 3 = W
54 **ACT** 2 = A, 1 = C and 9 = T
55–60 Refer to pages 25–30 on Substitution, Number and Logic, and pages 43–45 on Alphabetical Order (Curveball Questions 1).
55–59 Arrange the words in a grid to make it easier to put them in the correct alphabetical order.

55 **lonely**

l	o	a	d	e	d
l	o	c	a	l	s
l	o	c	k	e	t
l	o	n	e	l	y
l	o	u	n	g	e

56 **march**

b	l	a	n	k
b	l	o	w	n
e	v	e	r	y
m	a	r	c	h
m	a	r	r	y

57 **rascal**

r	a	t	t	l	e
r	a	s	c	a	l
r	a	i	s	i	n
r	a	f	f	l	e
r	a	c	k	e	t

58 **square**

s	u	p	e	r	b
s	q	u	a	r	e
s	p	r	e	a	d
s	p	o	k	e	n
s	p	l	i	n	t

59 **puppets**

p	u	r	p	o	s	e
p	u	p	p	e	t	s
f	o	r	e	i	g	n
c	o	n	c	e	r	t
c	o	l	l	e	c	t

60 Use the drawing to help get the answer. The Blacks, Greys and Whites live on the even side of South Street, thus the Greys must live in 4 as they are between the other two, and we know the Browns live in 1.

If the Greens live opposite the Blacks, the Blacks must live in 6 with the Greens in 5. This means the Whites live in 2 and the Blues in the remaining house, number 3, which is a higher number than the Whites in number 2.

1 Browns	3 Blues	5 Greens
2 Whites	4 Greys	6 Blacks

1–5 Refer to pages 8–11 on Synonyms.
1 **bend, curve** Both words mean an arch shape.
2 **small, slight** Both words means little or slender.
3 **ruin, destroy** Both words mean spoil or devastate.
4 **author, writer** Both words indicate someone who writes.
5 **fast, swift** Both words mean rapid.
6–10 Refer to pages 15–19 on Finding Words and Letters.
6 **BAG** cabbages
7 **ONE** honest
8 **APE** paper
9 **MAT** tomatoes
10 **OAT** throat
10–15 Refer to pages 20–24 on Sorting Words and Letters.
11 **have**
12 **throb**
13 **core**
14 **rope**
15 **sand**
16–20 Refer to pages 15–19 on Finding Words and Letters.
16 **hiss** I don't like the clothes in **this s**hop.
17 **mash** The cine**ma sh**ows new films each week.
18 **stir** Running around help**s tir**e you out.
19 **meat** There's been an accident; co**me at** once!
20 **romp** Jade received letters **from p**eople she had never heard of.
21–25 Refer to pages 31–34 on Word Progressions.
21 **e** far, cane
22 **p** soil, peat
23 **i** host, paint
24 **a** hunt, laid
25 **r** dear, sport
26–35 Refer to pages 20–24 on Sorting Words and Letters.
26–30 Try each of the words in the first set of brackets. Do they make sense with any words in the second and third sets of brackets? Only one combination of three words makes sense.
26 **school, important, wonders**
27 **found, umbrella, rain**
28 **fire, building, quickly**
29 **cat, black, collar**
30 **drank, put on, left**
31 The **weather** is **better** now.
32 I'm **looking** forward to **supper**.
33 I like **the** book you gave **me**.
34 **Do** try to clean it **up**.
35 I **knocked** over the **vase**.
36–40 Refer to pages 39–42 on Sequences.
36 **D79** The letter in the first group moves forwards one place in the second group. The number in the first group decreases by 1 in the second group.
37 **G20** The letter in the first group moves forwards one place in the second group. The number in the first group stays the same in the second group.
38 **F18** The letter in the first group moves forwards one place in the second group. The number in the first group increases by 3 in the second group.
39 **GH8** Each letter in the first group moves forwards two places in the second group. The number in the first group increases by 1 in the second group.

40 QRS Each letter in the first trio moves forwards two places in the second trio.

41–45 Refer to pages 12–14 on Antonyms.

41 still, active 'Still' means motionless whereas 'active' means moving about.

42 warm, cool 'Warm' is the direct opposite of 'cool' as they are on their way to being hot or cold respectively, whereas hot is the opposite of cold or freezing the opposite of boiling.

43 bend, straighten 'Bend' means to curve whereas 'straighten' means to uncurl.

44 fix, destroy To 'fix' means to mend whereas to 'destroy' means to obliterate.

45 low, high 'Low' means short or close to the ground whereas 'high' means tall or a long way from the ground.

46–50 Refer to pages 25–30 on Substitution, Number and Logic and pages 43–45 on Alphabetical Order (Curveball Question 1). Arrange the words in a grid to make it easier to put them in the correct alphabetical order.

D	N	A	L	R	A	G
E	L	B	M	A	G	
P	O	L	L	A	G	
R	E	T	H	A	G	
T	I	B	M	A	G	

46 garland
47 gallop
48 g, a
49 gallop
50 6 Each word has one except for 'garland' which has two.

51–54 Refer to pages 35–38 on Codes. The easiest way to complete this type of question is to put the letters in a grid:

g	h	b	j	k	l	m
D	E	T	A	I	N	S

51 lhjb N = l, E = h, A = j and T = b
52 ghlb D = g, E = h, N = l and T = b
53 DEAN g = D, h = E, j = A and l = N
54 STAIN m = S, b = T, j = A, k = I and l = N

55–59 Refer to pages 20–24 on Sorting Words and Letters.

55 guests A party would not exist without 'guests'.
56 coat A dog must have a furry 'coat'.
57 food A restaurant is a business that sells 'food'.
58 a steering wheel A car can exist without all the other words except 'a steering wheel'.
59 rules A board game may have all the things mentioned but games definitely have 'rules'.

60–65 Refer to pages 39–42 on Sequences.

60 add, reduce 'Add' is the same as 'combine'; 'reduce' is the same as 'subtract'.
61 lose, tie 'Fail' is the same as 'lose'; 'draw' is the same as 'tie'.
62 catch, free 'Trap' is the same as 'catch'; 'release' is the same as 'free'.
63 give, accept 'Donate' is the same as 'give'; 'receive' is the same as 'accept'.
64 command, request 'Order' is the same as 'command'; 'ask' is the same as 'request'.
65 delete, circle 'Erase' is the same as 'delete'; 'ring' is the same as 'circle'.

Mixed Paper 3

1–5 Refer to pages 12–14 on Antonyms. To complete this type of question, try the first word with the rest, then the second with the rest and so on.

1 lead, iron These other words are verbs for moving.
2 mountain, hill The other words are bodies of water.
3 cross, angry These are negative feelings. The other words are positive feelings.
4 sun, moon The other words are colours.
5 rest, sleep The other words are related to weather.

6–10 Refer to pages 15–19 on Finding Words and Letters.

6 NOW snowing
7 VAN servant
8 EAR early
9 RIM primroses
10 RAT scratch

11–15 Refer to pages 20–24 on Sorting Words and Letters.

11 bluebell
12 sunshine
13 footstep
14 afterwards
15 football

16–20 Refer to pages 15–19 on Finding Words and Letters.

16 pour My mother makes us kee<u>p our</u> house tidy.
17 calf I like juice made from tropi<u>cal f</u>ruits.
18 chap Ea<u>ch ap</u>ple costs forty-nine pence.
19 lint After all those years, I was sti<u>ll int</u>erested in it.
20 etch Despite losing I don't regr<u>et ch</u>anging.

21–25 Refer to pages 31–34 on Word Progressions.

21 s team, keys
22 o flat, hero
23 s tall, skin
24 r bead, fore
25 r pint, rate

26–30 Refer to pages 20–24 on Sorting Words and Letters. Try each of the words in the first set of brackets. Do they make sense with any words in the second and third set of brackets? Only one combination of three words makes sense.

26 tried, son, homework
27 sign, road, stop
28 plane, sky, flying
29 walked, quickly, castle
30 highwaymen, coach, gold

31–35 Refer to pages 39–42 on Sequences. When completing this type of question, it is worth remembering that the next letter after Z will be A as the alphabet will start again.

31 NP Each letter in the first pair moves forwards four places in the second pair.
32 YZ Each letter in the first pair moves back four places in the second pair.
33 MOQ Each letter in the first trio moves forwards one place in the second trio.
34 DW The first letter in the first pair moves forwards one place in the second pair. The second letter in the first pair moves back one place in the second pair.
35 FGE The first letter in the first trio moves forwards one place in the second trio. The second letter stays the same. The third letter in the first trio moves back one place in the second trio.

36–39 Refer to pages 25–30 on Substitution, Number and Logic.

36

O	R	B	I	T
R	■	R	■	A
G	■	A	■	I
A	N	V	I	L
N	■	E	■	S

37

P		C		L
O	C	H	R	E
R		E		A
T	U	S	K	S
S		T		T

38

C	A	G	E	D
H				A
E	L	D	E	R
E				E
R	O	P	E	S

39

P	U	N	C	H
		I		U
S	I	G	H	S
		H		K
S	A	T	E	S

40–44 Refer to pages 20–24 on Sorting Words and Letters.
  40 <u>fruit</u>, **meat** If you don't eat fish or meat you are a vegetarian.
  41 <u>draw</u>, **wear** In a car you should always wear a seat belt.
  42 <u>read</u>, **eat** In Chinese restaurants many people eat with chopsticks.
  43 <u>stars</u>, **crosses** Noughts and crosses is a fun game to play with friends.
  44 <u>hot</u>, **windy** It was so windy last night that a tree in our garden was blown over.
45–49 Refer to pages 35–38 on Codes. Start with SOW as it is the only three-letter word, therefore SOW = 562. WHOSE is the only five-letter word, therefore WHOSE = 27651. ROSE is the only four lettered word not starting with 'S', therefore ROSE = 8651. Once you know these three, you can deduce the rest. So, SHOE = 5761 and SHOW = 5762.
  45 **5761** S = 5, H = 7, O = 6, E = 1
  46 **27651** W = 2, H = 7, O = 6, S = 5, E = 1
  47 **562** S = 5, O = 6, W = 2
  48 **5762** S = 5, H = 7, O = 6, W = 2
  49 **8651** R = 8, O = 6, S = 5, E = 1
50–54 Refer to pages 39–42 on Sequences.
  50 **evening, morning** 'Dusk' is when the light fades in the 'evening' as 'dawn' is when the sun comes up in the 'morning'.
  51 **ordinary, unusual** 'Common' is the same as 'ordinary' as 'unique' is the same as 'usual'.
  52 **swift, steady** 'Sudden' is the same as 'swift' as 'gradual' is the same as 'steady'.
  53 **tilted, vertical** 'Leaning' is the same as 'tilted' as 'upright' is the same as 'vertical'.
  54 **ride, walk** All the words could apply here but the link is that you 'ride' a 'horse' and 'walk' a 'dog'.
55–56 Refer to pages 25–30 on Substitution, Number and Logic.
  55 **9** 2 + 3 + 4 = 9
  56 **3** (4 + 5) ÷ 3 = 9 ÷ 3 = 3
57–61 Refer to pages 15–19 on Finding Words and Letters.

  57 **y** many, yawn; day, yet
  58 **p** trap, pea; hop, pit
  59 **n** dawn, note; main, nun
  60 **s** pass, saw; was, sty
  61 **d** bead, dry; bed, dew
62–64 Refer to pages 8–11 on Synonyms.
  62 **trout**
  63 **home**
  64 **mist**

Mixed Paper 4

1–5 Refer to pages 12–14 on Antonyms. Category A is animals. (**ferret, baboon, mole**)
Category B contains words to do with buildings or structures. (**bridge, arcade, cinema**)
Category C contains tools. (**drill, saw**)
Category D contains colours. (**rose, beige**)
6–10 Refer to pages 12–14 on Antonyms. Try the first word from the first set of brackets with each word in the second set of brackets. Repeat this method with the second and third words from the first set of brackets, until you find the correct combination.
  6 **break, mend** To 'break' is to damage, whereas to 'mend' is to repair.
  7 **stretch, shrink** To 'stretch' is to make larger whereas to 'shrink' is to make smaller.
  8 **empty, full** 'Empty' has nothing in it whereas 'full' means complete.
  9 **plentiful, scarce** 'Plentiful' means there is a lot of something whereas 'scarce' means there is very little.
  10 **winner, loser** A 'winner' is someone who succeeds. A 'loser' is someone who fails.
11–15 Refer to pages 15–19 on Finding Words and Letters.
  11 **b** numb, bread
  12 **e** pipe, ever
  13 **s** toss, soak
  14 **y** play, yell
  15 **t** that, tint
16–20 Refer to pages 20–24 on Sorting Words and Letters.
  16 **stain** There is no 's', 'i' or 'n' in 'terrace'.
  17 **stead** There is no 'e' in 'distant'.
  18 **tramp** There is no 'm' in 'painter'.
  19 **ages** There is no 's' in 'general'.
  20 **clean** There is no 'n' in 'clearest'.
21–25 Refer to pages 15–19 on Finding Words and Letters.
  21 **alto** Going to the seaside is an ide<u>al to</u>nic.
  22 **idea** The cup is bes<u>ide a</u> bunch of flowers.
  23 **hare** Her teet<u>h are</u> white and beautifully clean.
  24 **seas** It means it i<u>s eas</u>y to control.
  25 **tour** We think tha<u>t our</u> ways are best.
26–30 Refer to pages 31–34 on Word Progressions.
  26 **HEAR** 27 **FARM**
  28 **BULK** 29 **WINE**
  30 **SENT**
31–35 Refer to pages 20–24 on Sorting Words and Letters. Try each of the words in the first set of brackets. Do they make sense with any words in the second and third set of brackets? Only one combination of three words makes sense.
  31 **sunny, woman, beach**
  32 **spring, green, lambs**
  33 **quickly, station, train**
  34 **boat, rock, water**

35 jumped, cold, swam

36–40 Refer to pages 8–11 on Synonyms.

36 lie A 'lie' means a fabrication (so is false or an unthruth); to 'lie' down is the same as to rest or lounge.

37 pack A 'pack' is another word for a group or gang, as well as meaning to put things into a container.

38 star A 'star' is a word associated with astronomy (like 'planet' and 'sun'); a 'star' is also a famous person, performer or celebrity.

39 kind 'Kind' means considerate and nice; it also means a type, sort or category of something.

40 cold 'Cold' is similar in meaning to 'cool' and 'chilly'; it is also associated with illness, like 'flu' and 'infection'.

41–44 Refer to pages 25–30 on Substitution, Number and Logic.

41

P	A	R	T	Y
A	■	■	O	■
P	A	I	N	T
E	■	■	I	■
R	E	A	C	T

42

H	O	L	D	S
I	■	■	■	H
P	A	T	I	O
P	■	■	■	U
O	N	S	E	T

43

P	L	U	C	K
E	■	■	■	N
R	A	D	I	O
C	■	■	■	T
H	O	O	P	S

44

C	R	A	Z	E
L	■	F	■	R
E	■	T	■	R
A	■	E	■	O
R	A	R	E	R

45–49 Refer to pages 39–42 on Sequences. When completing this type of question, it is worth remembering that the next letter after Z will be A as the alphabet will start again.

45 DP FU The first letter in each pair follows the repeating sequence D, E, F. The second letter in each pair moves forwards one place each time.

46 8R 4T The number in each group decreases by half each time. The letter in each group moves forwards two places each time.

47 CB FC The first letter in each group moves forwards one place each time. The second letter in each pair follows the sequence A A B B C C.

48 8A 5Z The number in each pair follows the sequence 8 5 8 5 8 5. The letter in each pair moves back one place each time.

49 FU EV The first letter in each pair moves back one place each time. The second letter in each pair moves forwards by one letter each time.

50–59 Refer to pages 35–38 on Codes.

50 ○ ◆ ❞ ① R = ○, A = ◆, T = ❞ and E = ①

51 ① ◆ ○ E = ①, A = ◆ and R = ○

52 TAG ❞ = T, ◆ = A and △

53 TEA ❞ = T, ① = E and ◆ = A

54 GREAT △ = G, ○ = R, ① = E, ◆ = A and ❞ = T

55–59 Start by writing out the first ten numbers of the alphabet and write the letters underneath them

1	2	3	4	5	6	7	8	9	10
A	B	C	D	E	F	G	H	I	J

55 8945

56 31754

57 FACED

58 HEDGED

59 BEACH

60–64 Refer to pages 25–30 on Substitution, Number and Logic.

60 act

61 belt

62 know

63 moor

64 sty

Curveball Questions 2: Sequences

1 AP, UB The first letter in each pair moves backwards one place. The second letter moves forwards two places.

2 AN, DW The first letter in each pair moves forwards one place. The second letter moves forwards three places.

3 4X7, 6T5 The first number in a trio increases by 1 each time. The letter in the middle of the trio moves back two places each time. The last number in the trio decreases by 1 each time.

4 B6, C13 The letters are in a sequence: A A B B C C. The number added increases by 1 each time: +1, +2, +3, +4, +5.

5 11, 19 The sequence alternately adds 8 and subtracts 6: +8, -6, +8, -6, +8.

6 CE, EK The first letter in the pair moves forwards one place each time. The second letter in the pair moves forwards three places each time.

7 ZA, QF The first letter in the pair moves back five places then forwards three places, repeating the pattern. The second letter in the pair moves forwards one place.

8 KM, MI The first letter in the pair moves forwards three places then back one place, repeating the pattern. The second letter in the pair moves back two places each time.

9 BC, FG Each letter in the first pair moves forwards four places in the following pair.

10 UP, CL The first letter in the pair moves forwards four places each time. The second letter in the pair moves back two places each time.

11 AD, EH Each letter in the first pair moves forwards four places in the second pair.

12 CV, IB Both letters move forwards two places

each time.

13 **96, 91** Each number in the sequence decreases by 5.

14 **72, 54** Each number in the sequence decreases by 9.

15 **17, 19** The number added decreases by 1 each time: +5, +4, +3, +2, +1.

16 **6.66, 0.666** The number is divided by 10 each time.

17 **16, 18** There are two sequences which alternate. In the first sequence, starting with 6, the number increases by 6 each time. In the second sequence, starting with 16, the number increases by 4 each time.

18 **3, 12** The number doubles each time.

19 **46, 47** The sequence alternately subtracts 5 and adds 1: −5, +1, −5, +1, −5, +1.

20 **16, 30** There are two sequences which alternate. For the first, third, fifth and seventh numbers, the number added increases by 1 each time: +4, +5, +6. For the second, fourth, sixth and eighth numbers, the number also increases by 1 each time: +5, +6, +7.

21 **11, 19** The sequence alternately adds 5 and subtracts 2: +5, −2, +5, −2, +5, −2, +5.

22 **22, 29** There are two sequences which alternate. In the first sequence starting with 7, the number added increases by 1 each time: +4, +5, +6. In the second sequence starting with 17, each number in the sequence increases by 4.

23 **4, 36** This is a sequence of squared numbers from 2^2 to 9^2.

24 **13, 17** The sequence alternately adds 2 and 4: +2, +4, +2, +4, +2, +4, +2.

25 **4, ½** The number halves each time.

Test Paper 1

1–5 Refer to pages 8–11 on Synonyms.
  1 **appreciation, thanks**
  2 **creak, squeak**
  3 **gallant, brave**
  4 **rubbish, litter**
  5 **silence, quietness**
6–10 Refer to pages 15–19 on Finding Words and Letters.
  6 **w** when, nettle
  7 **r** fear, rubber
  8 **d** sword, delight
  9 **m** stem, mount
  10 **d** sound, dawn
11–15 Refer to pages 12–14 on Antonyms.
  11 **even** An 'odd' number is 1, 3, 5 and so on. An 'even' number is 2, 4, 6 and so on.
  12 **deep** 'Shallow' means of no great depth whereas 'deep' means going a long way down.
  13 **part** The 'whole' means all of something, whereas a 'part' means a section of something.
  14 **joyful** 'Sad' is miserable whereas 'joyful' is happy.
  15 **end** To 'start' is to begin whereas to 'end' is to finish.
16–20 Refer to pages 31–34 on Word Progressions. When a letter appears more than once, try out different combinations until you find a real word.
  16 **TRAP**

		1		2	3	4					1		2	3	4	

C	O	M	B		A	L	E	S			P	A	R	T		R	A	P	S

  17 **TEAM**

	1	2	3	4					1	2	3	4	
W	I	D	E		S	K	I	P		S	I	T	E		A	M	P	S

  18 **DRAG**

2	4?1?	3 4?1?		2	4?1?	3 4?1?
O	P	E	N		S	E	N	T		R	A	I	D		A	G	U	E

  19 **STEM**

4?	1 2?	3?2?4?3?		4?	1 2?	3?2?4?3?
S	A	G	E		T	E	S	T		M	A	S	T		T	O	N	E

  20 **PORT**

1 (2/3)(2/3)	(2/3) 4		1 (2/3)(2/3)	(2/3) 4
F	R	E	E		S	E	A	L		S	P	O	T		F	R	E	T

21–25 Refer to pages 20–24 on Sorting Words and Letters.
  21 **nothing**   **22** **carpet**   **23** **landmark**
  24 **another**   **25** **bedstead**
26–30 Refer to pages 15–19 on Finding Words and Letters.
  26 **leap** A sing<u>le ap</u>ple is very good for you.
  27 **skin** Thi<u>s kin</u>d of behaviour is useless.
  28 **tall** To speak like that isn'<u>t all</u>owed.
  29 **farm** You will need to write that <u>far m</u>ore neatly.
  30 **tool** Come quickly or you will be <u>too l</u>ate.
31–35 Refer to pages 31–34 on Word Progressions.
  31 **BAKE**   **32** **MARK**   **33** **MAKE**
  34 **LONG**   **35** **COLT**
36–40 Refer to pages 20–24 on Sorting Words and Letters.
  36 Do **you** want to **borrow** it?
  37 Where **are** your **shoes**?
  38 I must **buy** a new **one**.
  39 **I'll** clean **it** tomorrow.
  40 I **hope** I'll get **full** marks.
41–45 Refer to pages 39–42 on Sequences.
  41 **finish, conclude** 'Finish' and 'conclude' are synonyms in the same way as 'depart' and 'leave'.
  42 **freeze, cool** You 'cool' something in order to 'freeze' it, in the same way as you 'warm' something in order to 'heat' it.
  43 **second, minute** A 'minute' is made up of 'seconds' in the same way as a 'pound' is made up of 'pence'.
  44 **ebb, flow** 'Find' and 'lose' are opposites in the same way as 'ebb' and 'flow' are.
  45 **noon, day** 'Noon' is the middle of the 'day' as 'midnight' is the middle of the 'night'.
46–50 Refer to pages 20–24 on Sorting Words and Letters.
  46 **money** A 'bank' is an institution that looks after 'money'.
  47 **a lens** A 'camera' must have 'a lens' to take pictures.
  48 **keys** A 'piano' must have 'keys' in order to work.
  49 **a seat** A 'chair' is not something to sit on unless it has 'a seat'.
  50 **child** In order to be a 'father' you must have a 'child'.
51–55 Refer to pages 35–38 on Codes.
  51 ” ○ ○ ① V = ”, E = ○ and R = ①
  52 ① ○ ◆ ① R = ①, E = ○ and A = ◆
  53 **GEAR** △ = G, ○ = E, ◆ = A and ① = R
  54 **EAGER** ○ = E, ◆ = A, △ = G and ① = R
  55 **GAVE** △ = G, ◆ = A, ” = V and ○ = E

56–67 Refer to pages 25–30 on Substitution, Number and Logic.

56 20 $6 + 5 + 5 + 4 = 20$
57 15 $3 + 1 + 6 + 5 = 15$
58 12 $2 + 5 + 1 + 4 = 12$
59 15 $6 + 1 + 3 + 5 = 15$
60 16 $4 + 5 + 1 + 6 = 16$

61–65 A table is the easiest way to sort the information, like this:

R	$100 - 4 = 96$
M	$\frac{1}{2}$ of $96 = 48$
G	$100 - 5 = 95$
D	$95 - 7 = 88$
S	$96 - 12 = 84$

61 R   **62 G**   **63 D**
64 S   **65 M**

66–67 Fire engines are red. This is supported by the information, 'My car is red; so are fire engines.' **Ford make cars.** This is supported by the information, 'My sister's car is a Ford.'

68–70 Refer to pages 20–24 on Sorting Words and Letters.
68 TEAR
69 HOSE
70 BEARD

71–77 Refer to pages 15–19 on Finding Words and Letters.
71 tree "It's Christmas Eve tomorrow!" shouted the children.
72 carrot The vegetables in our allotment are amazing.
73 storm The waves crashed angrily onto the beach.
74 n neat, none, nice, note
75 t tail, tape, tear, there
76 f fact, flag, fall, face
77 h hair, hail, hand, hold

78–80 Refer to pages 8–11 on Synonyms.
78 chuckle   **79 irregular**   **80 terminate**

Test Paper 2

1–5 Refer to pages 20–24 on Sorting Words and Letters.
1 summer, winter Winter is my favourite season because I love it when it snows.
2 newspapers, invitations I sent out invitations to everyone I wanted to come to my birthday party.
3 sings, reads My mother reads out a story to me before bed each night.
4 monkey, lion The lion is known as the king of the jungle.
5 flower, tree Elm, oak and maple are all types of tree.

6–10 Refer to pages 12–14 on Antonyms.
6 front, back 'Front' is the side facing outwards whereas 'back' is the rear of something.
7 rough, smooth 'Smooth' means flat or even whereas 'rough' is uneven or bumpy.
8 bent, straight 'Bent' is crooked whereas 'straight' is in an unbending line.
9 sell, buy When you 'buy' something you part with money; when you 'sell' something you receive money.
10 here, there 'Here' means positioned close to you whereas 'there' is away from you.

11–15 Refer to pages 31–34 on Word Progressions.

11 hose   **12 raps**   **13 warm**
14 this   **15 seat**

16–25 Refer to pages 15–19 on Finding Words and Letters.
16 rain rainbow, raindrop, rainfall, raincoat
17 fire fireguard, firefly, firework, fireplace
18 tooth toothache, toothbrush, toothpaste, toothpick
19 road roadshow, roadworks, roadblock, roadworthy
20 moon moonstruck, moonbeam, moonlight, moonstone
21 news For his birthday, I got Dad <u>new s</u>ocks.
22 then The <u>ne</u>xt time he snaps, I'm going!
23 hear The <u>ar</u>t teacher was unwell today.
24 duet She missed her turn <u>due t</u>o long queues.
25 fund Areas of path on the cliff <u>und</u>er our feet were slippery.

26–30 Refer to pages 31–34 on Word Progressions. Use grids, as shown below, to help work out the missing words.

26 FREE

1	2			3	4		1	2			3	4	
C	O	D	E	F	A	S	T	F	R	O	G	G	L	E	E

27 DEAD

	3?	1/4		2	3?	1/4			3?	1/4		2	3?	1/4
D	E	C	K	S	I	C	K	K	I	N	D	L	E	A	D

28 ISLE

	1?	2		1?		3	4		1?	2		1?		3	4
O	P	E	N	P	O	T	S	D	I	S	K	A	B	L	E

29 BRAT

	2	3?	1?	4	3?	1?			2	3?	1?	4	3?	1?	
C	L	A	P	N	A	P	E	C	R	A	B	T	A	S	K

30 BARK

	3/4	2	1	3/4				3/4	2	1	3/4			
S	L	I	P	L	O	U	D	D	R	A	B	K	N	O	W

31–35 Refer to pages 20–24 on Sorting Words and Letters.
31 Do **you** live on the High **Street**?
32 It is **hot** and the flowers are **wilting**.
33 I've **used** all the **paper** already.
34 The **cat** slept **blissfully** in the sun.
35 I feel **sick in** a car.

36–40 Refer to pages 8–11 on Synonyms.
36 answer 'Reply' and 'answer' both mean to respond.
37 find 'Discover' and 'find' both mean to locate something.
38 study 'Examine' and 'study' both mean to look closely at.
39 believe 'Trust' and 'believe' both mean to have faith in.
40 lengthy 'Long' and 'lengthy' both mean of some duration.

41–50 Refer to pages 25–30 on Substitution, Number and Logic.

41

Y	E	A	R	S
■		P	■	Y
S	U	P	E	R
■		L	■	U
B	L	E	E	P

42

L	E	M	O	N
A	■	U	■	■
S	E	N	S	E
S	■	C	■	■
O	T	H	E	R

43

S	H	E	L	L
■	■	A	■	A
N	I	G	H	T
■	■	E	■	H
T	H	R	E	E

44

S	C	O	R	E
A	■	P	■	■
B	R	E	A	K
L	■	N	■	■
E	A	S	E	L

45

C	R	O	W	D
L	■	T	■	R
E	■	H	■	E
A	R	E	N	A
R	■	R	■	R

46–50 Refer to pages 25–30 on Substitution, Number and Logic and pages 43–45 on Alphabetical Order (Curveball Question 1). Arrange the words in a grid to make it easier to put them in the correct alphabetical order.

46 REASON

R	E	A	D	Y		
R	E	A	L	I	S	E
R	E	A	S	O	N	
R	E	B	E	L		
R	E	C	K	O	N	

47 SCARED

S	A	F	E	T	Y	
S	A	I	L	O	R	
S	C	A	R	E	D	
S	C	E	N	E		
S	C	H	E	M	E	

48 DELIVER

D	E	L	E	T	E	
D	E	L	I	G	H	T
D	E	L	I	V	E	R
D	E	P	E	N	D	
D	E	P	R	E	S	S

49 CHASE

C	H	A	O	S		
C	H	A	R	T		
C	H	A	S	E		
C	L	I	F	F		
C	L	O	S	E		

50 BOAST

B	L	A	N	K		
B	L	A	R	E		
B	O	A	S	T		
B	O	I	L	I	N	G
B	R	A	W	L		

51–55 Refer to pages 35–38 on Codes. Start with REACH as that is the only five-letter word that does not begin with 'C'. The code for this must be 0 4 3 1 ✦. You also know that the two four lettered words start with 'P', so P = △. All the others can subsequently be worked out.

51 1 ✦ 3 0 7 C = 1, H = ✦, A = 3, R = 0 and T = 7

52 1 ✦ 4 3 △ C = 1, H = ✦, E = 4, A = 3 and P = △

53 △ 4 3 0 P = △, E = 4, A = 3 and R = 0

54 △ 3 0 7 P = △, A = 3, R = 0 and T = 7

55 0 4 3 1 ✦ R = 0, E = 4, A = 3, C = 1 and H = ✦

56–65 Refer to pages 15–19 on Finding Words and Letters.

56 k drink, know; flick, kite

57 b stub, bun; flab, bat

58 e tile, eyes; slime, ends

59 n worn, nose; plan, newt

60 l meal, light; fill, lost

61 bare　　　　**62 main**　　　　**63 raft**

64 cover　　　　**65 short**

66–68 Refer to pages 8–11 on Synonyms.

66 valiant　　　　**67 liberty**　　　　**68 arrogant**

69–72 Refer to pages 35–38 on Codes. 'BOOM' has a double letter. There are no repeated letters in the codes you were given so the missing code is for 'BOOM'. 'BOMB' has a repeated letter at the beginning and end of the word so it must match 'x 9 F x'. From this you can work out all the codes.

69 x 9 9 F B = x, O = 9, O = 9, M = F

70 9 F 3 & O = 9, M = F, E = 3, N = &

71 x 9 F x B = x, O = 9, M = F, B = x

72 MOON F = M, 9 = O, 9 = O, & = N

73–80 Refer to pages 15–19 on Finding Words and Letters.

73 by It is important to plant trees.

74 in Children should play outside more.

75 sky Low flying aircraft are very noisy.

76 where What will you be wearing tonight?

77 snow snowstorm, snowball, snowplough, snowman

78 hand handout, handbook, handcuff, handshake

79 water waterfall, waterproof, watertight, watercolour

80 under underground, underline, understand, underarm